Food Dudes

MILTON HERSHEY:

Hershey's Chocolate Creator

Joanne Mattern

Checkerboard Library

An Imprint of Abdo Publishing
www.abdopublishing.com

www.abdopublishing.com

Published by Abdo Publishing, a division of ABDO, PO Box 398166, Minneapolis, Minnesota 55439.
Copyright © 2015 by Abdo Consulting Group, Inc. International copyrights reserved in all countries.
No part of this book may be reproduced in any form without written permission from the publisher.
Checkerboard Library™ is a trademark and logo of Abdo Publishing.

Printed in the United States of America, North Mankato, Minnesota.
052014
092014

J·B
HERSHEY
63-9784

Cover Photos: Alamy; Corbis
Interior Photos: Alamy pp. 16–17, 17, 19, 26; Corbis pp. 1, 24; Courtesy of Hershey Community
    Archives, Hershey, PA pp. 4, 5, 7, 8, 9, 11, 13, 15, 18, 21, 23, 27; North Wind p. 12

Series Coordinator: BreAnn Rumsch
Editors: Megan M. Gunderson, BreAnn Rumsch
Art Direction & Cover Design: Neil Klinepier

Library of Congress Control Number: 2014941020

Mattern, Joanne, 1963-
  Milton Hershey : Hershey's chocolate creator / Joanne Mattern.
     p. cm. -- (Food dudes)
  ISBN 978-1-62403-494-7
  1. Hershey, Milton Snavely, 1857-1945--Juvenile literature. 2. Hershey Foods Corporation--
History--Juvenile literature. 3. Businessmen--United States--Biography--Juvenile literature. 4.
Chocolate industry--United States--History--Juvenile literature. 5. Chocolate candy--United States--
History--Juvenile literature. I. Title.
  HD9200.U52H475 2015
  338.7'66392092--dc23
  [B]
                                     2014941020

Contents

Life on the Farm

Milton Hershey learned strong values from his mother, Fanny. They contributed to his success later in life.

Who doesn't love chocolate? It is delicious in cookies, on ice cream, or by itself! Yet just 100 years ago, few Americans even knew what this tempting treat tasted like. Milton Hershey changed everything when he created the Hershey bar. For the first time, delicious, sweet chocolate was available to anyone who wanted it.

Milton Snavely Hershey was born on September 13, 1857. His life began on a farm called the Homestead. It was near Hockersville, Pennsylvania. His parents were Henry and Veronica "Fanny" Hershey. Milton had a younger sister named Serena.

Both Henry and Fanny had grown up in **Mennonite** families. Fanny

The Homestead later served an important role during Milton's journey to success.

embraced that lifestyle. She valued hard work and determination. Still, the family never had much money. Henry worked on the farm during Milton's early days. But, he changed jobs often. Whenever Henry got a new job, the family had to move.

In 1866, the family settled on a farm near Lancaster, Pennsylvania. But life soon became more difficult than ever. The next year, Serena died. This loss upset Milton's parents greatly. Fanny blamed Henry for their troubles. Eventually, she told him to leave.

Off to Work

Milton's troubled family life and constant moving made it difficult for him to become educated. He first attended Derry Church School. By the time he was 13, he had attended six other schools!

In 1870, Milton quit school. He had only a fourth grade education. In those days, many children left school early to work. Like them, Milton had to help support his family.

The next year, Milton was **apprenticed** to a printer named Sam Ernst. Unfortunately, Milton's lack of reading skills made this job difficult. He was also clumsy. After just three months, Ernst lost patience with Milton and let him go.

In 1872, Milton's mother apprenticed him to Joseph R. Royer. Royer owned Royer's Ice Cream Parlor and Garden in Lancaster. His shop also sold candy. Royer taught Milton how to make many kinds of candy. Finally, Milton had a job he really liked!

By the time he was 18, Milton had learned much from Royer. In fact, Milton felt ready to open his own candy store. However, he did not have enough money to do this. So, Milton borrowed $150 from his mother's family. He then opened a taffy shop in Philadelphia, Pennsylvania. Milton was proud to be running his own business.

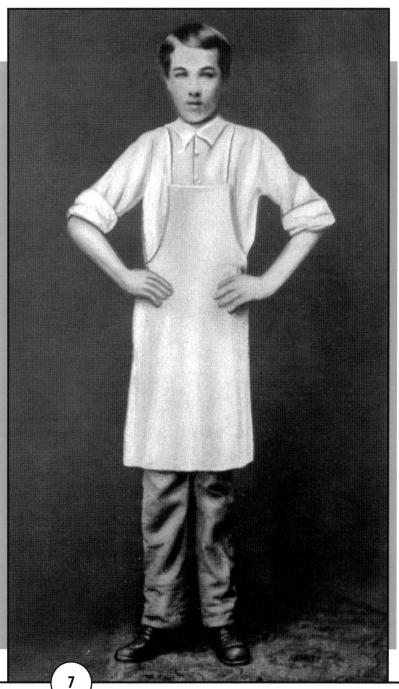

Milton had a natural talent for making candy.

Candy Man

Milton's father heard of his son's start in the candy business. Henry was always full of business ideas. So, he traveled to Philadelphia to share them with Milton. Henry's advice was not good. Milton worked hard, but he did not make much money.

After six years in business, Milton's candy shop failed. Milton felt ashamed. So in 1882, he moved away to Denver, Colorado. There, he got a job with a candy maker.

The candy maker taught Milton how to make caramels. At that time, most caramels contained **paraffin**. Yet in Denver, Milton learned of a secret ingredient that made his caramels delicious. Fresh milk instead of paraffin made the candies taste wonderful. They stayed fresh longer, too.

Henry had always dreamed of being an inventor. Milton went on to follow this dream for himself.

Armed with this knowledge, Milton moved to Chicago, Illinois. He started a business there making caramel candies. But, he didn't stay for long. In 1883, Milton moved to New York City, New York. During the day, he worked for a candy maker. At night, he made his own caramels. But, sales were slow. In 1886, he moved back to Lancaster to start over one more time.

Caramel King

Back in Pennsylvania, Hershey started the Lancaster Caramel Company. One day in 1887, an Englishman visited the town. He tasted some of Hershey's caramels and thought they were delicious. The man offered to introduce Hershey's caramels to people in London, England.

There was just one problem. Hershey would have to produce more caramels than ever! To do this, Hershey needed to expand his factory. So, he went to the bank and got a loan from Frank Brenneman.

Then, Hershey went to work making caramels. But when his loan came due, Hershey had not yet finished filling orders for London. In fact, he needed even more money to get the job done.

Hershey wanted Brenneman to see how his loan was invested. So, he invited the banker to visit the factory. Brenneman liked what he saw there and believed Hershey could be successful. So, Brenneman lent Hershey some of his own money. The money allowed Hershey to fill his orders in time. As soon as the Englishman paid him, Hershey rushed to the bank and paid off his **debts**.

People liked Hershey's caramels, so his sales increased. By the 1890s, Hershey had finally achieved success as a candy maker. He became one of Lancaster's most important citizens.

Hershey opened more factories as his caramel business grew. By 1900, he employed more than 1,500 people.

Chocolate Dreams

Hershey was fascinated by inventions. So, he loved attending events such as the World's Columbian Exposition.

Most Americans living during the late 1800s had never heard of chocolate. The first time Hershey saw chocolate being made was in 1893 at the World's Columbian Exposition. This gathering of exhibits was held in Chicago, Illinois. One exhibit displayed some special machines from Germany. They were used to make chocolate.

When Hershey tasted what the chocolate-making machines had created, he felt inspired. He wanted to start a new business making chocolate. In the past, chocolate had been expensive to make. So, only wealthy people had been able to buy it. But Hershey wanted to make chocolate a treat that everyone could afford to enjoy.

Hershey bought the German chocolate equipment and put it in his caramel factory in Lancaster. There, Hershey experimented until he found the right method for making his chocolate. He began using the chocolate to coat his caramels. He also produced cocoa powder and unsweetened baking chocolate. Hershey was on his way to great success.

It takes many steps to turn cocoa beans into chocolate. At the factory, cocoa bean roasters are the first machines used in the process.

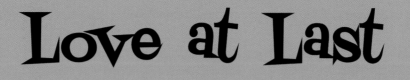

Love at Last

In 1894, Hershey started the Hershey Chocolate Company. The company made fancy chocolates that came in many different shapes. Hershey made his first chocolate sale in April 1895.

Even though Hershey kept busy with work, he was often lonely. That changed in 1897. While traveling in New York, Hershey met Catharine "Kitty" Sweeney at a sweets shop. Kitty worked at the ribbon counter at Altman's department store in New York City.

On Sundays, Hershey took the train from Pennsylvania to New York to visit Kitty. The two quickly fell in love. Then on May 25, 1898, they married.

The Hersheys loved spending time together. They traveled a lot and often went to the theater. They also gave many parties and enjoyed visiting with their friends. Hershey had never been happier.

Kitty was a loving, supportive wife. She encouraged her husband to follow his heart when making business decisions.

Sweet Success

Meanwhile, Hershey wanted to figure out how to make milk chocolate. This treat was a guarded secret in Europe, so there were no recipes to follow! Hershey moved his chocolate equipment to the farm where he had been born. There at the Homestead, he could work in secret.

Hershey spent years working on his recipe. Eventually, his hard work and countless attempts paid off. Hershey was the first American to develop a milk chocolate formula.

In 1900, Hershey introduced the milk chocolate Hershey bar. This treat only cost consumers five cents. At first, the chocolate spoiled quickly. So, the bars were only sold in Lancaster.

Today's chocolate-making process has not changed from the original.

Eventually, Hershey's company perfected its milk chocolate formula. Soon, Hershey bars were sold all around the country.

Hershey's chocolate business grew so successful that he needed to expand his operation. So, Hershey began looking for a new factory

location. He thought it would be best to be close to Pennsylvania's dairy farms. That would make it easier to get all the milk he needed for his chocolate.

Hershey realized he was more interested in chocolate than in caramel. So in August 1900, he sold the Lancaster Caramel Company for $1 million. That was

a huge amount of money in those days! Hershey would soon invest it all into building his chocolate empire.

After Hershey perfected his milk chocolate formula, more products emerged. Hershey's Kisses debuted in 1907. Hershey's Syrup was first sold in 1926.

Chocolate Town

In 1902, Hershey bought 1,200 acres (490 ha) of land near the Homestead in the Pennsylvania countryside. He planned to build a new chocolate factory there. The next year, construction began. The new factory was completed in 1905.

Around the factory, Hershey constructed a town called Hershey. On a hill above the chocolate factory, he built his new home. The mansion was called High Point.

Hershey built his factory in the heart of Pennsylvania's dairy farming country. There, it was close to one of milk chocolate's most important ingredients, milk!

In those days, many factory owners built towns for their workers. But those towns were usually plain and not much fun to live in.

Hershey's town was different. He provided his workers with nice homes. He also built excellent schools for their children.

Hershey believed workers did their jobs better if they were treated fairly and lived comfortably. He wanted his employees to be happy and eager to work. So, everything they needed was available in the town. There were churches, stores, a post office, and a bank.

The town also had plenty of places to have fun. These included parks, golf courses, and a zoo. A **trolley** system moved

Today, Hershey residents and tourists enjoy the many public spaces Hershey planned.

people about town. In 1907, Hershey built an amusement park for his workers. It was called Hershey Park. In was renamed Hersheypark in 1971.

Hershey's School

The Hersheys loved children, so they decided to help those in need. On November 15, 1909, Hershey established the Hershey Industrial School. He invited orphaned boys to attend the school. Hershey knew what it was like to grow up with very little. He wanted to help these boys have a good life.

The next year, the school **enrolled** its first four boys. They began to live and attend classes in the Homestead. Hershey Industrial School students were given nice clothes to wear and good food to eat. All the boys learned to read, write, do mathematics, and run the farm. They also learned a useful trade, which helped them find work when they left school. And when they graduated, each boy received $100.

The Hersheys were very happy to help the boys. They never had any **biological** children. So, Hershey said he "decided to make the orphan boys of the United States my heirs."

Hershey always made time for the Industrial School boys.

Called to Cuba

In 1910, Mrs. Hershey became ill with a nerve disease. She could no longer walk, and she even had trouble breathing. Hershey took good care of his wife. And, he brought her flowers every day. Sadly, Mrs. Hershey's health grew worse. On March 23, 1915, she died.

After his wife's death, Hershey began spending a lot of time away from home. He was drawn to Cuba's warm weather. In addition, he knew Cuba's plantations could provide his business with a very important ingredient. Chocolate could not be made without sugar.

Until that time, Hershey had imported his sugar from Europe. Yet when **World War I** began there, it became difficult to get a full supply. So in 1916, Hershey purchased 65,000 acres (26,300 ha) of Cuban sugarcane fields. He also opened a sugar **refinery** there.

Hershey wanted his Cuban workers to be just as happy as his Pennsylvania workers were. So, he built them a town called Central Hershey. It had nice homes, parks, and schools. In 1925, Hershey opened the Hershey Agricultural School for orphaned boys.

At its height, Hershey's Cuban operation employed nearly 4,000 people. His sugar refinery was the largest on the island at the time.

Central Hershey houses had electricity and running water.
These luxuries were a first for most Cuban workers at that time.

Hershey's contributions benefited the local **economy**. For this, the Cuban government granted him the Grand Cross of the National Order in 1933. It is the highest honor a foreigner can earn from Cuba.

After the war, sugar was once again available in the United States. Yet Hershey's Cuban operation continued for several years. Then in 1946, it was sold to the Cuban Atlantic Sugar Company.

A Giving Heart

Through his businesses in Pennsylvania and Cuba, Hershey became a very wealthy man. He believed it was important to use that wealth to help others. So as early as 1905, Hershey established the Hershey Trust Company. This group manages the funds for Hershey's many charitable efforts.

More than 600 local workers were employed to build the Hotel Hershey.

24

In 1918, Hershey put the Hershey Trust Company in charge of $60 million. This was almost his entire fortune. All the money would benefit the Hershey Industrial School. Today, that fund is worth more than $6 billion.

Hershey's school was renamed the Milton Hershey School in 1951. Today, it offers education to about 1,800 boys and girls each year. The school provides these students with important opportunities. Many graduates go on to enjoy successful careers.

During the **Great Depression**, Hershey wanted to give jobs to people in need. So, he paid workers to build the Hotel Hershey. This luxury hotel opened on May 26, 1933. Workers also built a sports stadium. With these additions, the town of Hershey became a popular travel destination.

In 1935, Hershey started the M.S. Hershey Foundation. Today, the foundation supports educational and **cultural** opportunities for people in the Hershey area. Its sites include the Hershey Gardens, the Hershey Theatre, and the Hershey Story museum.

Living On

Hershey's chocolate sales continued to grow each year. During **World War II**, Hershey invented a survival chocolate bar for soldiers. It was called the Ration D bar. By the end of the war, more than 1 billion were produced!

On October 13, 1945, Milton Hershey died in Hershey Hospital. Today, Hershey's business lives on. The company was renamed Hershey Foods Corporation in 1968. But today, it is called the Hershey Company. It manufactures many chocolates, candies, and other foods. These products are exported to more than 90 countries.

From chocolate treats to Reese's Pieces, Twizzlers, and Jolly Ranchers, Hershey's has something for every sweet tooth!

The company's success has allowed Hershey's trust to continue enriching the community. In 1963, the trust gave land and $50 million to Pennsylvania State University's College of Medicine. The college started a hospital called Milton S. Hershey Medical Center. It is a leading health care facility that helps thousands of people each year.

Milton Hershey was a poor boy, but he worked hard to be successful. Then he used his wealth to help others. Today, he is known all over the world for his delicious candy and for all he did to make life better for other people.

Hershey continues to be recognized as a man with a vision and an open heart.

Timeline

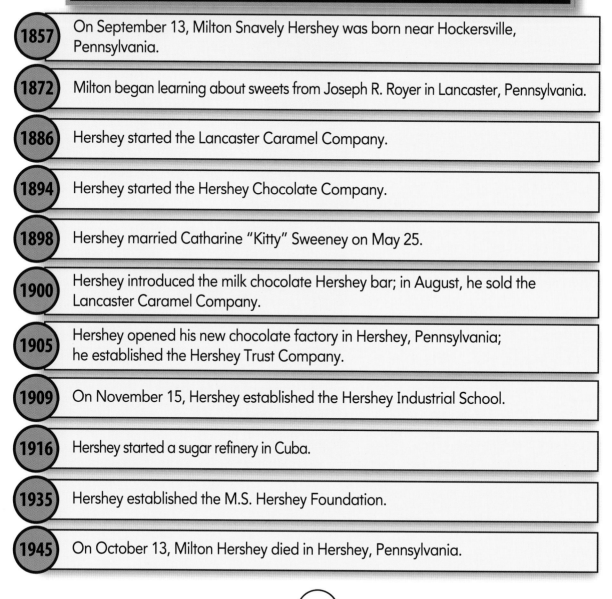

1857 On September 13, Milton Snavely Hershey was born near Hockersville, Pennsylvania.

1872 Milton began learning about sweets from Joseph R. Royer in Lancaster, Pennsylvania.

1886 Hershey started the Lancaster Caramel Company.

1894 Hershey started the Hershey Chocolate Company.

1898 Hershey married Catharine "Kitty" Sweeney on May 25.

1900 Hershey introduced the milk chocolate Hershey bar; in August, he sold the Lancaster Caramel Company.

1905 Hershey opened his new chocolate factory in Hershey, Pennsylvania; he established the Hershey Trust Company.

1909 On November 15, Hershey established the Hershey Industrial School.

1916 Hershey started a sugar refinery in Cuba.

1935 Hershey established the M.S. Hershey Foundation.

1945 On October 13, Milton Hershey died in Hershey, Pennsylvania.

Funky Flavor

Chocolate has been around for thousands of years! Over time, people have created many distinctive flavors from this special food.

It wasn't until 1875 that milk chocolate was first created by German Henri Nestlé. Manufacturers around Europe began trying to imitate the popular new treat.

Without knowing Nestlé's exact process, manufacturers created varied methods. As a result, different flavors of milk chocolate emerged in different places. Around Europe, milk chocolate may be milky, rich, dark, or caramelized.

Hershey's milk chocolate is the first ever made in America. His recipe produces a slightly sour chocolate. Yet, Americans love it! That is because people tend to prefer the flavor of the chocolate they grew up eating.

Do you know what chocolate flavor you like best?

Glossary

apprentice - to bind someone as an apprentice. An apprentice is someone who learns a trade or a craft from a skilled worker.

biological - connected by a relationship involving genes rather than adoption or marriage.

cultural - of or relating to the customs, arts, and tools of a nation or a people at a certain time.

debt - something owed to someone, especially money.

economy - the way a nation produces and uses goods, services, and natural resources.

enroll - to register, especially to attend a school.

Great Depression - the period from 1929 to 1942 of worldwide economic trouble. There was little buying or selling, and many people could not find work.

Mennonite - a member of one of the Protestant religious groups founded in Holland in the 1500s. Mennonites are noted for dressing plainly and living simply.

paraffin - a waxy substance used in candles, medicines, and makeup.

refinery - the building and machinery used for purifying products such as sugar or petroleum.

trolley - a device used to carry electricity to a streetcar or an electric engine.

World War I - from 1914 to 1918, fought in Europe. Great Britain, France, Russia, the United States, and their allies were on one side. Germany, Austria-Hungary, and their allies were on the other side.

World War II - from 1939 to 1945, fought in Europe, Asia, and Africa. Great Britain, France, the United States, the Soviet Union, and their allies were on one side. Germany, Italy, Japan, and their allies were on the other side.

Websites

To learn more about Food Dudes, visit **booklinks.abdopublishing.com**. These links are routinely monitored and updated to provide the most current information available.

Index